To SAMARA. JAN - 2017
wishing yo ⟡ W9-BYD-879
1 FAR Ahead and on the
Success in your life

SUCCESS

101

WHAT EVERY LEADER NEEDS TO KNOW

JOHN C. MAXWELL

THOMAS NELSON
Since 1798

NASHVILLE   DALLAS   MEXICO CITY   RIO DE JANEIRO   BEIJING

Published in Nashville, Tennessee, by Thomas Nelson. Thomas Nelson is a registered trademark of Thomas Nelson, Inc.

Published in association with Yates & Yates, www.yates2.com

Thomas Nelson, Inc., titles may be purchased in bulk for educational, business, fund-raising, or sales promotional use. For information, please e-mail SpecialMarkets@ThomasNelson.com.

Portions of this book have been previously published in *Your Road Map for Success*, *Failing Forward*, *The 360° Leader*, *Winning with People*, *The 21 Indispensable Qualities of a Leader*, and *The 17 Essential Qualities of a Team Player* by John C. Maxwell.

Library of Congress Cataloging-in-Publication Data

Maxwell, John C., 1947–
    Success 101 : what every leader needs to know / John C. Maxwell.
        p. cm.
    ISBN 978-1-4002-8023-0
    1. Success in business--Handbooks, manuals, etc. I. Title.
HF5386.M4449 2008
658.4'09--dc22

                                                    2008026082

Printed in the United States of America

12 QG 10

Contents

PREFACE

I've been passionate about personal growth for most of my life. In fact, I've created and pursued a plan for growth every year for the last forty years! People say that wisdom comes with age. I don't believe that's true. Sometimes age comes alone. I wouldn't have achieved any of my dreams had I not been dedicated to continual improvement. If you want to grow and become the best person you can be, you've got to be intentional about it.

At the same time, life is busy and complex. Most people run out of day long before their to-do list is done. And trying to get to the bottom line in just about any area of life can be a challenge. Did you know that more new information has been produced in the last thirty years than in the previous five thousand? A single weekday edition of the *New York Times* contains more information than most people in seventeenth-century England were likely to encounter in their lifetimes.

That's why we've developed this series of 101 books. We've cherry-picked the essentials in subjects such as leadership, attitude, relationships, teamwork, and mentoring and put them into a format that you very likely can read in one sitting. Or you can easily toss a 101 book into a briefcase or purse and read here and there as time allows.

In many of my larger books, I go into my subject in great depth. I do that because I believe it is often the best way to add value to people. *Success 101* is different. It is an introduction to a subject, not the "advanced course." But I believe it will help you on your way to significant growth in this area of your life.

I hope you enjoy this book, and I pray that it serves you well as you seek to improve your life and achieve your dreams.

PART 1

THE RIGHT PICTURE OF SUCCESS

I

WHAT IS SUCCESS?

You cannot achieve what you have not defined.

The problem for most people who want to be successful is not that they can't achieve success. The main obstacle for them is that they misunderstand success. Maltbie D. Babcock said, "One of the most common mistakes and one of the costliest is thinking that success is due to some genius, some magic, something or other which we do not possess."

THE TRADITIONAL PICTURE OF SUCCESS

What is success? What does it look like? Most people have a vague picture of what it means to be a successful person that looks something like this:

The wealth of Bill Gates,
the physique of Arnold Schwarzenegger
   (or Marilyn Monroe),

the intelligence of Albert Einstein,

the athletic ability of Michael Jordan,

the business prowess of Donald Trump,

the social grace and poise of Jackie Kennedy,

the imagination of Walt Disney, and

the heart of Mother Teresa.

That sounds absurd, but it's closer to the truth than we would like to admit. Many of us picture success as looking like one other than who we are—and we especially can't be eight other people! And more important than that, you shouldn't want to be. If you tried to become just like even one of these other people, you wouldn't be successful. You would be a bad imitation of them, and you would eliminate the possibility of becoming the person you were meant to be.

THE RIGHT PICTURE OF SUCCESS

So how do you get started on the journey toward success? What does it take to be a success? Two things are required: the right picture of success and the right principles for getting there.

The picture of success isn't the same for any two people because we're all created differently as unique individuals. But the process is the same for everyone. It's based on principles that do not change. After more than thirty-five years of knowing successful people and studying the subject, I have developed the following definition of success:

Success is . . .
Knowing your purpose in life,
Growing to reach your maximum potential, and
Sowing seeds that benefit others.

You can see by this definition that success is a journey rather than a destination. No matter how long you live or what you decide to do in life, you will never exhaust your capacity to grow toward your potential or run out of opportunities to help others. When you see success as a journey, you'll never have the problem of trying to "arrive" at an elusive final destination. And you'll never find yourself in a position where you have accomplished some final goal, only to discover that you're still unfulfilled and searching for something else to do.

Another benefit of focusing on the journey of success

instead of on arriving at a destination or achieving a goal is that you have the potential to become a success *today*. The very moment that you make the shift to finding your purpose, growing to your potential, and helping others, successful is something you *are right now*, not something you vaguely hope one day to be.

To get a better handle on these aspects of success, let's take a look at each one of them:

KNOWING YOUR PURPOSE

Nothing can take the place of knowing your purpose. Millionaire industrialist Henry J. Kaiser, the founder of Kaiser Aluminum as well as the Kaiser-Permanente health care system, said, "The evidence is overwhelming that you cannot begin to achieve your best unless you set some aim in life." Or put another way, if you don't try actively to discover your purpose, you're likely to spend your life doing the wrong things.

I believe that God created every person for a purpose. According to psychologist Viktor Frankl, "Everyone has his own specific vocation or mission in life. Everyone must carry out a concrete assignment that demands fulfillment. Therein he cannot be replaced, nor can his life be repeated.

Thus everyone's task is as unique as his specific opportunity to implement it." Each of us has a purpose for which we were created. Our responsibility—and our greatest joy—is to identify it.

Here are some questions to ask yourself to help you identify your purpose:

For what am I searching? All of us have a strong desire buried in our hearts, something that speaks to our deepest thoughts and feelings, something that sets our souls on fire. Some people have a strong sense of what that is when they're just children. Others take half a lifetime to discover it. But no matter what, it's there. You only need to find it.

Why was I created? Each of us is different. No one else in the world has exactly the same gifts, talents, background, or future. That's one of the reasons it would be a serious mistake for you to try to be someone other than yourself.

Think about your unique mix of abilities, the resources available to you, your personal history, and the opportunities around you. If you objectively identify these factors and discover the desire of your heart, you will have done a lot toward discovering your purpose in life.

Do I believe in my potential? You cannot consistently act in a manner inconsistent with the way you see yourself. If you don't believe that you have potential, you will never try to reach it. And if you aren't willing to work toward reaching your potential, you will never be successful.

You should take the advice of President Theodore Roosevelt, who said, "Do what you can, with what you have, where you are." If you do that with your eyes fixed on your life purpose, what else can be expected of you?

When do I start? Some people live their lives from day to day, allowing others to dictate what they do and how they do it. They never try to discover their true purpose for living. Others know their purpose, yet never act on it. They are waiting for inspiration or permission or an invitation to get started. But if they wait much longer, they'll never get going. So the answer to the question "When do I start?" is NOW.

GROWING TO YOUR POTENTIAL

Novelist H. G. Wells held that wealth, notoriety, place, and power are no measures of success whatsoever. The only true measure of success is the ratio between what we might have been and what we have become. In other words, success comes as the result of growing to our potential.

It's been said that our potential is God's gift to us, and

what we do with it is our gift to him. But at the same time, our potential is probably our greatest untapped resource. Henry Ford observed, "There is no man living who isn't capable of doing more than he thinks he can do."

We have nearly limitless potential, yet too few ever try to reach it. Why? The answer lies in this: We can do *anything*, but we can't do *everything*. Many people let everyone around them decide their agenda in life. As a result, they never really dedicate themselves to *their* purpose in life. They become a jack-of-all-trades, master of none—rather than a jack-of-few-trades, focused on one.

If that describes you more than you'd like, you're probably ready to take steps to make a change. Here are four principles to put you on the road to growing toward your potential:

1. Concentrate on One Main Goal. Nobody ever reached her potential by scattering herself in twenty directions. Reaching your potential requires focus. That's why it's so important for you to discover your purpose. Once you've decided where to focus your attention, you must decide what you are willing to give up to do it. And that's crucial. There can be no success without sacrifice. The two go hand in hand. If you desire to accomplish little, sacrifice little.

But if you want to accomplish great things, be willing to sacrifice much.

2. Concentrate on Continual Improvement. David D. Glass, chief executive officer of Wal-Mart stores, was once asked whom he admired most. His answer was Wal-Mart founder Sam Walton. He remarked, "There's never been a day in his life, since I've known him, that he didn't improve in some way." Commitment to continual improvement is the key to reaching your potential and to being successful. Each day you can become a little bit better than you were yesterday. It puts you one step closer to your potential. And you'll also find that what you *get* as the result of your growth is not nearly as important as what you *become* along the way.

3. Forget the Past. My friend Jack Hayford, founding pastor of Church on the Way in Van Nuys, California, commented, "The past is a dead issue, and we can't gain any momentum moving toward tomorrow if we are dragging the past behind us." Unfortunately, that's what too many people do; they drag the past with them wherever they go. And as a result, they never make any progress.

I like the attitude of Cyrus Curtis, who once owned the *Saturday Evening Post*. He had a sign hanging in his office that announced, "Yesterday ended last night." It was his way of reminding himself and his employees that the past is done, and we should be looking forward, not back.

Maybe you've made a lot of mistakes in your life, or you've had an especially difficult past with many obstacles. Work your way through it and move on. Don't let it prevent you from reaching your potential.

If you need inspiration, think of other people who overcame seemingly insurmountable obstacles, such as Booker T. Washington. He was born into slavery and was denied access to the resources available to white society, but he never let that prevent him from pursuing his potential. He founded the Tuskegee Institute and the National Black Business League. He said, "I have learned that success is to be measured not so much by the position that one has reached in life as by the obstacles which one has overcome while trying to succeed."

Think of Helen Keller, who lost her sight and hearing at nineteen months old. Helen overcame her severe disabilities, went on to graduate from Radcliffe College, and became an author, noted lecturer, and champion for people who are blind.

Think of Franklin Delano Roosevelt. In 1921, at the age of thirty-nine, he had a severe case of polio, which left him disabled and in terrible pain. He never walked again without assistance. But he didn't let that stop him from pursuing his potential. Eight years later, he became the governor of New York, and in 1932, he was elected president of the United States.

No doubt, you can think of others who have overcome tragedies or past mistakes to pursue their potential. You may even know personally some people who fought back from adversity to become successful. Let them inspire you. No matter what you've faced in the past, you have the *potential* to overcome it.

4. Focus on the Future. Baseball Hall of Famer Yogi Berra declared, "The future isn't what it used to be." Although that may be true, it's still the only place we have to go. Your potential lies ahead of you—whether you're eight, eighteen, forty-eight, or eighty. You still have room to improve yourself. You can become better tomorrow than you are today. As the Spanish proverb says, "He who does not look ahead remains behind."

SOWING SEEDS THAT BENEFIT OTHERS

When you know your purpose in life and are growing to reach your maximum potential, you're well on your way to being a success. But there is one more essential part of the journey: helping others. Without that aspect, the journey can be a lonely and shallow experience.

It's been said that we make a living by what we get, but we make a life by what we give. Physician, theologian, and philosopher Albert Schweitzer stated it even more strongly: "The purpose of human life is to serve, and to show compassion and the will to help others." For him, the journey of fulfilling his purpose led to Africa, where he served people for many years.

For you, sowing seeds that benefit others probably won't mean traveling to another country to serve the poor—unless that is the purpose you were born to fulfill. (And if it is, you won't be satisfied until that's what you're doing.) However, if you're like most people, helping others is something you can do right here at home, whether it's spending more time with your family, developing an employee who shows potential, helping people in the community, or putting your desires on hold for the sake of your team at work. The key is to find your purpose and help others while you're pursuing it. Entertainer Danny Thomas insisted that "all of us are born for a reason, but all of us don't discover why. Success in life has nothing to do with what you gain in life or accomplish for yourself. It's what you do for others."

The journey toward success and fulfillment will not look the same for everyone because the picture of success is different for every person. But the principles used to take the journey don't change. They can be applied at home, in school, at the office, on the ball field, and in church. That's what the remainder of this book is about—the principles that can help you work toward knowing your purpose, growing to your potential, and sowing seeds that benefit others. It doesn't matter where you are now. You can learn and apply these ideas. You can be successful today.

2

WHAT DIRECTION SHOULD I GO?

You will never go farther than your dreams take you.

If you live in a town near the ocean, you may have seen advertisements for "cruises to nowhere." Maybe you've even been on one. People get on board a cruise ship, and when they leave the pier, instead of setting out for a lush island or other exotic location, they go out to sea and travel in circles for a couple of days. Meanwhile they dine on sumptuous meals, lounge around the pool, enjoy the shows, and participate in onboard activities. It's similar to checking into a fine hotel or resort.

The problem for a lot of people is that their lives are too much like those cruises. They're on a trip with no set destination, no charted course. They're in a holding pattern, and they occupy their time pursuing pleasures or engaging in activities that don't have any lasting benefit. Meanwhile, they travel in circles. In the end, they finish no better than they started. A cruise to nowhere may be a fun way to occupy a few days of vacation time, but it's no way to spend your life.

As I mentioned before, success is a journey. You don't suddenly become successful when you arrive at a particular place or achieve a certain goal. But that doesn't mean you should travel without identifying a destination. You can't fulfill your purpose and grow toward your potential if you don't know what direction you should be going. You need to identify and sail toward your destination. In other words, you need to discover your dream.

THE POWER OF A DREAM

I believe that each of us has a dream placed in the heart. I'm not talking about wanting to win the lottery. That kind of idea comes from a desire to escape our present circumstances, not to pursue a heartfelt dream. I'm talking about a vision deep inside that speaks to the very soul. It's the thing we were born to do. It draws on our talents and gifts. It appeals to our highest ideals. It sparks our feelings of destiny. It is inseparably linked to our purpose in life. The dream starts us on the success journey.

When I look for the name of a person who identified

and lived out his dream, I think of auto industry pioneer and visionary Henry Ford. He asserted, "The whole secret of a successful life is to find out what it is one's destiny to do, and then do it."

Ford's dream grew out of his interest in anything mechanical. From boyhood, he had a passion for studying and tinkering with machinery. He taught himself about steam engines, clocks, and combustion engines. He traveled around the countryside doing repair work for free, just so he could get his hands on machines. He became a mechanic and watchmaker. He even worked as a night engineer for the Detroit Edison Company.

Ford became increasingly intrigued by the idea of the automobile, and he devoted more and more of his attention to it. In 1896, he built his first car in a shed behind his house. After that, he continued to think about how to improve his early efforts, and he studied the work of other car builders, including that of Ransom E. Olds, who manufactured the first Oldsmobile in 1900.

Out of his love for machinery and intrigue over the automobile grew Ford's dream: the creation of an inexpensive mass-produced automobile. Until then, the new horseless carriage had been an expensive luxury item, available to only the rich. But Ford was determined to put the automobile within the reach of the common person. In 1899, he helped form the Detroit Motor Company. But when his fellow organizers balked at the idea of manufacturing their product inexpensively in order to sell it to the masses, he left the company. However, he held on to his dream, and his efforts finally paid off. In 1903, he organized the Ford Motor Company and began to produce the Model T. The first year his new company produced just under 6,000 cars. But only eight years later, they produced more than 500,000. And they managed to reduce the initial retail price from $850 to only $360. Ford's dream became a reality.

Ford has been called a genius and has been credited with the birth of the assembly line and mass production. But no matter what he had going for him, his greatest asset was his dream and his willingness to devote himself to it.

A dream does many things for us:

A DREAM GIVES US DIRECTION

Have you ever known a person who didn't have a clue concerning what she wanted in life, yet was highly successful? I haven't either. We all need something worthwhile to aim for. A dream provides us with that. It acts as a compass, telling us the direction we should travel. And until we've identified that right direction, we'll never know for sure that our movement is actually progress. Our actions are just as likely to take us backward instead of forward. If you move in *any* direction other than toward your dream, you'll miss out on the opportunities necessary to be successful.

A DREAM INCREASES OUR POTENTIAL

Without a dream, we may struggle to see potential in ourselves because we don't look beyond our current circumstances. But with a dream, we begin to see ourselves in a new light, as having greater potential and being capable of stretching and growing to reach it. Every opportunity we meet, every resource we discover, every talent we develop, becomes a part of our potential to grow toward that dream. The greater the dream, the greater the potential. E. Paul Hovey said, "A blind man's world is bounded by the limits of his touch; an ignorant man's world by the limits of his knowledge; a great man's world by the limits of his vision." If your vision—your dream—is great, then so is your potential for success.

A DREAM HELPS US PRIORITIZE

A dream gives us hope for the future, and it also brings us power in the present. It makes it possible for us to prioritize everything we do. A person who has a dream knows what he is willing to give up in order to go up. He is able to measure everything he does according to whether or not it contributes to the dream, concentrating his attention on the things that bring him closer to it and giving less attention to everything that doesn't.

Ironically, many people do exactly the opposite. Rather than focus on their one dream and let go of the less important things, they want to keep every option open. But when they do, they actually face more problems because decision making becomes overly complicated for them. They are like a performer who spins plates. You might have seen one of those acts on an old television variety program such as *The Ed Sullivan Show*. The performer puts a plate on top of a long, thin rod and spins it. As long as the plate is spinning, it balances on the end of the rod. He then places the rod in a device so that it stands on end. Then he does the same thing with another rod and plate, and then another. He keeps adding plates until he has a whole bunch of them spinning. As he goes, he must occasionally stop, run back, and put more spin on the previous plates so that they don't fall.

A performer who is really good at this can get quite a few plates spinning very quickly in the beginning. But as time goes by, even the good ones find it harder to make any progress adding new plates because they're spending all their time going back to keep the previous ones spinning. Getting that last plate up and spinning usually takes an incredibly long time.

Keeping all your options open is a lot like that. At first, it's fun to have so many possibilities open before you. It seems to be an excellent idea. But as time goes by, you can't make any progress because you spend all your time preserving the options rather than moving forward.

When you have a dream, you don't have that problem. You can expend your time and energy only on the "plates" that bring you closer to your dream. You can allow all the others to stop spinning and crash to the floor. They are unimportant. That knowledge frees up your time to concentrate on the few things that make a difference, and it keeps you on the right track.

A DREAM ADDS VALUE TO OUR WORK

A dream puts everything we do into perspective. Even the tasks that aren't exciting or immediately rewarding take on added value when we know they ultimately contribute to the fulfillment of a dream. Each activity becomes an important piece in that bigger picture. It reminds me of the story of a reporter who talked to three construction workers pouring concrete at a building site. "What are you doing?" he asked the first worker. "I'm earning a paycheck," he grumbled.

The reporter asked the same question of a second laborer, who looked over his shoulder and said, "What's it look like I'm doing? I'm pouring concrete."

Then he noticed a third man, who was smiling and whistling as he worked. "What are you doing?" he asked the third worker.

He stopped what he was doing and said excitedly, "I'm building a shelter for the homeless." He wiped his hands clean on a rag and then pointed, "Look, over there is where the kitchen will be. And that over there is the women's dormitory. This here . . ."

Each man was doing the same job. But only the third was motivated by a larger vision. The work he did was fulfilling a dream, and it added value to all his efforts.

Vince Lombardi stated, "I firmly believe that any man's finest hour—his greatest fulfillment to all he holds dear—is that moment when he has worked his heart out in a good cause and lies exhausted on the field of battle—victorious." A dream provides the perspective that makes that kind of effort possible.

A DREAM PREDICTS OUR FUTURE

Katherine Logan said, "A vision foretells what may be ours. It is an invitation to do something. With a great mental picture in mind we go from one accomplishment to another, using the materials about us only as stepping-stones to that which is higher and better and more satisfying. We thus become possessors of the unseen values which are eternal."

When we have a dream, we're not just spectators sitting back hoping that everything turns out all right. We're taking an active part in shaping the purpose and meaning of our lives. And the winds of change don't simply blow us here and there. Our dream, when pursued, is the most likely predictor of our future. That doesn't mean we have any guarantees, but it does increase our chances for success tremendously.

WHERE WILL YOUR DREAM TAKE YOU?

Dare to dream and act on that dream. Do it in spite of problems, circumstances, and obstacles. History is filled with men and women who faced adversity and achieved success in spite of it. For example, the Greek orator Demosthenes stuttered! The first time he tried to make a public speech, he was laughed off the rostrum. But he had a dream of being a notable speaker. He pursued that dream and grew toward his potential. It is said that he used to put pebbles in his mouth and practice speaking over the sound of the crashing surf at the seashore. His persistence paid off. He lived his dream: he became the greatest orator of the ancient world.

Others dared to dream and became successes. Napoleon, despite humble parentage, became an emperor. Beethoven brought to life his inner vision for music when he composed symphonies, even after he lost his hearing. Charles Dickens dreamed of becoming a writer and became the most-read novelist in Victorian England—despite being born into poverty.

Oliver Wendell Holmes noted, "The great thing in this world is not so much where we are but in what direction we are moving." This is also one of the great things about having a dream. You can pursue your dream no matter where you are today. And what happened in the past isn't as important as what lies ahead in the future. As the saying goes, "No matter what a person's past may have been, his future is spotless." You can begin pursuing your dream today!

3

WHAT ROLE DOES FAILURE
PLAY IN SUCCESS?

You will not succeed unless you are willing to fail.

Too many people believe the process of achieving success is supposed to be easy. The great American inventor Thomas Edison observed that attitude among people. And this is how he responded to it:

> Failure is really a matter of conceit. People don't work hard because, in their conceit, they imagine they'll succeed without ever making an effort. Most people believe that they'll wake up some day and find themselves rich. Actually, they've got it half right, because eventually they do wake up.

Each of us has to make a choice. Are we going to sleep life away, avoiding failure at all costs? Or are we going to wake up and realize this: Failure is simply a price we pay to achieve success.

FAILURE IS NOT . . .

If you can change your perspective on failure, it will help you to persevere—and ultimately achieve your desires. So how should you judge failure? By taking a look at seven things failure is *not*:

1. PEOPLE THINK FAILURE IS AVOIDABLE . . . IT'S NOT

Everybody fails, errs, and makes mistakes. You've heard the saying "To err is human, to forgive divine." Alexander Pope wrote that more than 250 years ago. And he was only paraphrasing a saying that was common 2,000 years ago, during the time of the Romans. Things today are the same as they were then: if you're a human being, you're going to make mistakes.

You're probably familiar with Murphy's Law and the Peter Principle. Recently I came across something called "Rules for Being Human." I think it describes well the state we're in as people:

Rule #1: You will learn lessons.

Rule #2: There are no mistakes—only lessons.

Rule #3: A lesson is repeated until it is learned.

Rule #4: If you don't learn the easy lessons, they get *harder.* (Pain is one way the universe gets your attention.)

Rule #5: You'll know you've learned a lesson when your actions change.

You see, writer Norman Cousins was right when he said, "The essence of man is imperfection." So know that you're going to make mistakes.

2. PEOPLE THINK FAILURE IS AN EVENT ... IT'S NOT

Growing up, I thought that success and failure came in a moment. The best example I can think of is taking a test. If you got an F, it meant you failed. But I've come to realize that failure is a process. If you flunk a test, it doesn't mean you just failed a one-time event. The F shows that you neglected the process leading up to the test.

Failure is like success. It's not someplace you arrive. Just as success is not a single event, neither is failure. Success or failure comes from how you deal with life along the way. Truly, no one can conclude that he's failed until he breathes his last breath. Until then, he's still in process and the jury is still out.

3. PEOPLE THINK FAILURE IS OBJECTIVE . . . IT'S NOT

When you err—whether you miscalculate crucial figures, miss a deadline, blow a deal, make a poor choice concerning your children, or otherwise fumble a ball—what determines whether that action was a failure? Do you look at the size of the problem it causes or the amount of money it costs you or your organization? Is it determined by how much heat you have to take from your boss or by the criticism of your peers? No. Failure isn't determined that way. The real answer is that *you* are the only person who can really label what you do a failure. It's subjective. Your perception of and response to your mistakes determine whether your actions are failure.

Did you know that entrepreneurs almost never get their first business off the ground? Or their second? Or their third? According to Tulane University business professor Lisa Amos, the average for entrepreneurs is 3.8 failures before they finally make it in business. They are not deterred by problems, mistakes, or errors. Why? Because they don't see setbacks as failure. They recognize that three steps forward and two steps back *still* equals one step forward. And as a result, they overcome average and become achievers.

4. PEOPLE THINK FAILURE IS THE ENEMY . . . IT'S NOT

Most people try to avoid failure like the plague. They're afraid of it. But it takes adversity to create success. Basketball coach Rick Pitino states it even more strongly: "Failure is good," he says. "It's fertilizer. Everything I've learned about coaching I've learned from making mistakes." People who see failure as the enemy are captive to those who conquer it. Herbert V. Brocknow believes "the fellow who never makes a mistake takes his orders from one who does." Observe any highly successful person, and you'll discover a person who doesn't see a mistake as the enemy. That is true in any endeavor. As musicologist Eloise Ristad said, "When we give ourselves permission to fail, we at the same time give ourselves permission to excel."

5. PEOPLE THINK FAILURE IS IRREVERSIBLE . . . IT'S NOT

There's an old saying in Texas: "It doesn't matter how much milk you spill as long as you don't lose your cow." In other words, mistakes are not irreversible. Keep everything in perspective. The problems come when you see only the spilled milk and not the bigger picture. People who see failure correctly take it in stride.

Mistakes don't make them want to give up.
Success doesn't make them think that they are set up.

Every event—whether good or bad—is just one small step in the process of living. Or as Tom Peters says, "If silly things were not done, intelligent things would never happen."

6. PEOPLE THINK FAILURE IS A STIGMA ... IT'S NOT

Mistakes are not permanent markers. I love the perspective of Senator Sam Ervin Jr. He remarked, "Defeat may serve as well as victory to shake the soul and let the glory out." That's the way we need to look at failure.

When you make mistakes, don't let them get you down. And don't let yourself think of them as a stigma. Make each failure a step to success.

7. PEOPLE THINK FAILURE IS FINAL ... IT'S NOT

Even what may appear to be a huge failure doesn't need to keep you from achieving. Take a look at the story of Sergio Zyman. He was the mastermind behind New Coke, something that marketing consultant Robert McMath sees as one of the greatest product failures of all time.[1] Zyman, who successfully introduced Diet Coke, believed that Coca-Cola needed to act boldly to reverse its twenty-year market decline against its rival Pepsi. His solution was to stop offering the drink that had been popular for nearly a hundred years, change the formula, and offer it as New Coke. The move was an abysmal failure that lasted seventy-nine days and cost the company about $100 million. People hated New Coke. And it caused Zyman to leave the company.

But Zyman's problems with New Coke didn't keep him down. In fact, he doesn't even see them as failure. Years later when asked if it was a mistake, Zyman answers, "No, categorically."

A failure? "No."

A blunder, a misstep, a bust? "Another word between bust and, uh, something else," he replies. "Now if you say to me, 'The strategy that you guys embarked on didn't work,' I'll say, 'Yeah, absolutely it didn't work. But the totality of the action ended up being positive.'" Ultimately, the return of Coca-Cola Classic made the company stronger.

Zyman's assessment was confirmed by Roberto Goizueta, the late chairman and chief executive of the Coca-Cola Company. He hired Zyman back at Coca-Cola in 1993.

"Judge the results," said Goizueta. "We get paid to produce results. We don't get paid to be right."[2]

EMBRACE FAILURE

How can you help yourself learn a new definition of failure and develop a different perspective concerning failure and success? By making mistakes. Chuck Braun of Idea Connection Systems encourages trainees to think differently through the use of a mistake quota. He gives each student a quota of thirty mistakes to make for each training session. And if a student uses up all thirty? He or she receives another thirty. As a result, the students relax, think of mistakes in a whole new light, and begin learning.

As you approach your next big project or assignment, give yourself a reasonable mistake quotient. How many mistakes should you expect to achieve? Twenty? Fifty? Ninety? Give yourself a quota and try to hit it before bringing the task to completion. Remember, mistakes don't define failure. They are merely the price of achievement on the journey toward success.

4

How Do I Get Started?

The first step toward success is leading yourself exceptionally well.

Have you ever worked with people who didn't lead themselves very well? We often think that self-leadership is about making good decisions every day, when the reality is that we need to make a few critical decisions in major areas of life and then manage those decisions day to day.

Here's a classic example of what I mean. Have you ever made a New Year's resolution to exercise? You probably already believe that exercise is important. Making a decision to do it isn't that hard, but managing that decision—and following through—is much more difficult. Let's say, for example, that you sign up for a health club membership the first week of January. When you sign on, you're excited. But the first time you show up at the gym, there's a mob of people. There are so many cars that police are directing traffic. You drive around for fifteen minutes, and finally find a parking place—four blocks away. But that's okay; you're there for exercise anyway, so you walk to the gym.

Then when you get inside the building, you have to wait to even get into the locker room to change. But you think, *That's okay. I want to get into shape. This is going to be great.* You think that until you finally get dressed and discover all the machines are being used. Once again you have to wait. Finally, you get on a machine—it's not the one you really wanted, but hey, you'll take it—and you exercise for twenty minutes. When you see the line for the shower, you decide to skip it, take your clothes, and just change at home.

On your way out, you see the manager of the club, and you decide to complain about the crowds. She says, "Don't worry about it. Come back in three weeks, and you can have the closest parking place and your choice of machines. Because by then, 98 percent of the people who signed up will have dropped out!"

It's one thing to decide to exercise. It's another to actually follow through with it. As everyone else drops out, you will have to decide whether you will quit like everyone else or if you will stick with it. And that takes self-management.

What Successful People Must Self-Manage

If you want to be successful and gain credibility with your boss and others, focus on taking care of business in these seven areas:

1. Manage Your Emotions

It's important for everybody to manage emotions. Nobody likes to spend time around an emotional time bomb who may "go off" at any moment. Leaders and other successful people know when to display emotions and when to delay them. Sometimes they show them so that their teammates can feel what they're feeling. It stirs them up. Is that manipulative? I don't think so, as long as people are doing it for the good of the team and not for their own gain. Because leaders see more than others and ahead of others, they often experience the emotions first. By letting the team know what you're feeling, you're helping them to see what you're seeing.

Other times leaders have to hold their feelings in check. In his book *American Soldier,* Gen. Tommy Franks wrote about a devastating incident that occurred in Vietnam when he was a junior officer and the example that was set for him in this area by Lt. Col. Eric Antilla, who put the men he commanded ahead of his own emotional needs:

> I studied Eric Antilla's eyes. I knew he was gripped by anguish, but he never let it show. We were at war; he was commanding troops in combat. And his quiet resolve in meeting this catastrophe gave us all strength. In an hour he would grieve, but now he stood rock solid. In war, it is necessary that commanders be able to delay their emotions until they can afford them.[1]

When I say that successful people should delay their emotions, I'm not suggesting that they deny them or bury them. The bottom line in managing your emotions is that you should put others—not yourself—first in how you handle and process them. Whether you delay or display your emotions should not be for your own gratification. You should ask yourself, *What does the team need?* not, *What will make me feel better?*

2. MANAGE YOUR TIME

Time management issues are tough, but they are especially difficult for people who are neither at the top or bottom of an organization. Leaders at the top can delegate.

Workers at the bottom usually punch a time clock. They get paid an hourly wage, and they do what they can while they're on the clock. People in the middle who are trying to be successful are often expected to put in long hours to get work done. Because of that, they need to manage their time well.

Time is valuable. Psychiatrist and author M. Scott Peck said, "Until you value yourself, you won't value your time. Until you value your time, you will not do anything with it." In *What to Do Between Birth and Death* (Wm. Morrow & Co., 1992), Charles Spezzano says that people don't pay for things with money; they pay for them with time. If you say to yourself, *In five years, I'll have put enough away to buy that vacation house*, then what you are really saying is that the house will cost you five years—one-twelfth of your adult life. "The phrase *spending your time* is not a metaphor," said Spezzano, "It's how life works."

Instead of thinking about what you do and what you buy in terms of money, instead think about them in terms of time. Think about it. What is worth spending your life on? Seeing your work in that light just may change the way you manage your time.

3. Manage Your Priorities

Most people are generalists. They know a lot about a lot of things. However, most successful individuals are highly focused. The old proverb is true: If you chase two rabbits, both will escape. So what should you do? You should still try to get yourself to the point where you can manage your priorities and focus your time in this way:

80 percent of the time—work where you are strongest

15 percent of the time—work where you are learning

5 percent of the time—work in other necessary areas

This may not be easy to achieve, but it is what you should strive for. If you have people working for you, try to give them the things you aren't good at but they are. Or if possible, trade some duties with your colleagues so that each of you is playing to your strength. Remember, the only way to move up from the middle is to gradually shift from generalist to specialist, from someone who does many things well to someone who focuses on a few things she does exceptionally well.

The secret to making the shift is often discipline. In *Good to Great*, Jim Collins wrote:

Most of us lead busy, but undisciplined lives. We have ever-expanding "to do" lists, trying to build momentum by doing, doing, doing—and doing more. And it rarely works. Those who build the good-to-great companies, however, made as much use of "stop doing" lists as the "to do" lists. They displayed a remarkable amount of discipline to unplug all sorts of extraneous junk.[2]

You must be ruthless in your judgment of what you should not do. Just because you like doing something doesn't mean it should stay on your to-do list. If it is a strength, do it. If it helps you grow, do it. If your leader says you must handle it personally, do it. Anything else is a candidate for your "stop doing" list.

4. Manage Your Energy

Some people have to ration their energy so that they don't run out. Up until a few years ago, that wasn't me. When people asked me how I got so much done, my answer was always, "High energy, low IQ." From the time I was a kid, I was always on the go. I was six years old before I realized my name wasn't "Settle Down."

Now that I'm past sixty, I do have to pay attention to my energy level. In *Thinking for a Change*, I shared one of my strategies for managing my energy. When I look at my calendar every morning, I ask myself, *What is the main event?* That is the one thing to which I cannot afford to give anything less than my best. That one thing can be for my family, my employees, a friend, my publisher, the sponsor of a speaking engagement, or my writing time. I always make sure I have the energy to do it with focus and excellence.

Even people with high energy can have that energy sucked right out of them under difficult circumstances. I've observed that leaders in the middle of an organization often have to deal with what I call "the ABCs energy-drain."

> *Activity Without Direction*—doing things that
>   don't seem to matter
> *Burden Without Action*—not being able to do
>   things that really matter
> *Conflict Without Resolution*—not being able to
>   deal with what's the matter

If you find that you are in an organization where you often must deal with these ABCs, then you will have to work extra hard to manage your energy well. Either that or you need to look for a new place to work.

5. MANAGE YOUR THINKING

Poet and novelist James Joyce said, "Your mind will give back to you exactly what you put into it." The greatest enemy of good thinking is busyness, If you find that the pace of life is too demanding for you to stop and think during your workday, then get into the habit of jotting down the three or four things that need good mental processing or planning that you can't stop to think about. Then carve out some time later when you can give those items some good think-time. That may be thirty minutes at home the same day, or you may want to keep a running list for a whole week and then take a couple of hours on Saturday. Just don't let the list get so long that it disheartens or intimidates you.

I encouraged readers in *Thinking for a Change* to have a place to think, and I wrote about the "thinking chair" I have in my office. I don't use that chair for anything else other than my think-time. I've discovered since the book's publication that I didn't explain clearly enough how to correctly use the thinking chair. People at conferences told me that they sat in their own thinking chairs and nothing happened. I explain to them that I don't sit in that thinking chair without an agenda, just hoping that a good idea hits me. What I usually do is think about the things I've jotted down because I couldn't think about them during a busy day. I take the list to my chair, put it in front of me, and give each item as much think-time as it needs. Sometimes I'm evaluating a decision I've already made. Sometimes I'm thinking through a decision I will have to make. Sometimes I'm developing a strategy. Other times I'm trying to be creative in fleshing out an idea.

I want to encourage you to try managing your thinking in this way. If you've never done it before, you will be amazed by the payoff. A minute of thinking is often more valuable than an hour of talk or unplanned work.

6. Manage Your Words

Legendary basketball coach John Wooden said, "Show me what you can do; don't just tell me what you can do." Successful people value action. And if they are going to stop what they're doing long enough to listen, the words they hear need to have value. Make them count.

In *The Forbes Scrapbook of Thoughts on the Business Life* (Triumph Books, 1995), Emile de Girardin is quoted as saying, "The power of words is immense. A well-chosen word has often sufficed to stop a flying army, to change defeat into victory, and to save an empire." If you wish to make sure that your words carry weight, then weigh them well. The good news is that if you manage your thinking and take advantage of focused think-time, you will probably see improvement in the area of managing your words too.

David McKinley, a successful leader in a large organization in Plano, Texas, told me a story about something that happened in his first job after graduate school. He was preparing to make an important call on someone, and he decided that he should ask the top leader to go with him. When they got there, David, in his enthusiasm, just wouldn't stop talking. He didn't give his leader a chance to do anything but watch until the very end of their visit.

As they returned to the car, David's boss told him, "I might as well have stayed at the office." He went on to explain how his presence was superfluous. David told me, "I learned a huge lesson that day about staying 'in bounds' when I was with the senior leader. His honest counsel and correction strengthened our relationship and has served me well throughout my life." If you have something worthwhile to say, say it briefly and well. If you don't, sometimes the best thing to do is remain silent.

7. Manage Your Personal Life

You can do everything right at work and manage yourself well there, but if your personal life is a mess, it will eventually turn everything else sour. What would it profit a person to climb to the top of the organizational chart but to lose a marriage or alienate the children? As someone who spent many years counseling people, I can tell you, no career success is worth it.

For years one of my definitions of *success* has been this: having those closest to me love and respect me the most. That is what is most important. I want the love and respect of my wife, my children, and my grandchildren before I want the respect of anyone I work with. Don't get me wrong. I want the people who work with me to respect me too, but not at the expense of my family. If I blow managing myself at home, then the negative impact will spill over into every area of my life, including work.

LEAD YOURSELF FIRST

If you want to influence others, you must always lead yourself first. If you can't, you have no credibility. That applies whether the influence you desire to exert is on the people above you, beside you, or below you. The better you are at making sure you're doing what you should be doing, the better chance you have for making an impact on others and being successful.

PART II

THE CORE QUALITIES FOR SUCCESS

5

How Well Do I
Work with People?

*It is no exaggeration to say that the ability to work with
people is the most important ingredient for success.*

What kind of price would you put on good people skills? Ask the successful CEOs of major corporations what characteristic is most needed for success in leadership positions, and they'll tell you it's the ability to work with people. Interview entrepreneurs to find out what separates the successes from the failures, and they'll tell you it is skill with people. Talk to top salespeople and they'll tell you that people knowledge is much more important than mere product knowledge. Sit down with teachers and tradesmen, shop foremen and small business owners, pastors and parents, and they'll tell you that people skills make the difference between those who excel and those who don't. People skills are invaluable. It doesn't matter what you want to do. If you can win with people, you can win!

WHAT KIND OF PERSON ARE YOU?

For years psychologists have attempted to divide people into various categories. Sometimes an observant poet can do a better job. Ella Wheeler Wilcox did so in the poem "Which Are You?"

There are two kinds of people on earth today;
Just two kinds of people, no more, I say.

Not the sinner and saint, for it's well understood,
That the good are half-bad and the bad half-good.

Not the rich and the poor, for to rate a man's wealth,
You must first know the state of his conscience and health.

Not the humble and proud, for in life's little span,
Who puts on vain airs, is not counted a man.

Not the happy and sad, for the swift flying years
Bring each man his laughter and each man his tears.

No; the two kinds of people on earth I mean,
Are the people who lift, and the people who lean.
Wherever you go, you will find the earth's masses,
Are always divided in just these two classes.

And oddly enough, you will find too, I ween,
There's only one lifter to twenty who lean.

In which class are you? Are you easing the load,
Of overtaxed lifters, who toil down the road?
Or are you a leaner, who lets others share
Your portion of labor, and worry and care?[1]

These are good questions we must ask ourselves, because our answers will have a huge impact on our relationships. I think Wilcox was on the right track. People do tend to add value to others, lessening their load and lifting them up, or they take away value from others, thinking only of themselves and taking people down in the process. But I would take that one step farther. I believe the intensity with which we lift or lower others can determine that there are really *four* kinds of people when it comes to relationships:

1. SOME PEOPLE ADD SOMETHING TO LIFE— WE ENJOY THEM

Many people in this world desire to help others. These people are adders. They make the lives of others more pleasant and enjoyable. They're the lifters Wilcox wrote about. Evangelist D. L. Moody advised people to . . .

do all the good you can,
to all the people you can,
in all the ways you can,
as long as ever you can.

Moody was an adder.

People who add value to others almost always do so *intentionally.* I say that because adding value to others requires a person to give of himself, and that rarely occurs by accident. I have endeavored to become an adder. I like people, and I want to help them. I make it my goal to be a friend.

Recently the CEO of a large corporation invited me to speak on leadership for his organization. After teaching his executives and conducting sessions for his managers, I had gained enough credibility with him that he wanted to do something nice for me.

"John, I like what you've done for us," he said as we sat one day in his office. "Now, what can I do for you?"

"Nothing," I replied. "You don't need to do anything for me." The corporation had, of course, paid me for the times I had spoken, and I had really enjoyed the experience. His people were sharp and eager to learn.

"Oh, come on," he said. "Everybody wants *something.* What do you want?"

"Look, doesn't everybody need an easy friend? Somebody who doesn't want anything?" I answered, looking him in the eye. "I just want to be an easy friend."

He chuckled and said, "Okay, you'll be my easy friend." And that's who I have endeavored to be. Author Frank Tyger says, "Friendship consists of a willing ear, an understanding heart and a helping hand." That's what I'm trying to give my friend.

2. SOME PEOPLE SUBTRACT SOMETHING FROM LIFE— WE TOLERATE THEM

In *Julius Caesar*, playwright William Shakespeare's Cassius asserts, "A friend should bear his friend's infirmities, But Brutus makes mine greater than they are." That's what subtracters do. They do not bear our burdens, and they make heavier the ones we already have. The sad thing about subtracters is that what they do is usually unintentional. If you don't know how to add to others, then you probably subtract by default.

In relationships, receiving is easy. Giving is much more difficult. It's similar to the difference between building something and tearing it down. It takes a skilled craftsman much time and energy to build a beautiful chair. It takes no skill whatsoever to smash that chair in a matter of moments.

3. SOME PEOPLE MULTIPLY SOMETHING IN LIFE— WE VALUE THEM

Anyone who wants to can become an adder. It takes only a desire to lift people up and the intentionality to follow through. That is what George Crane was trying to teach his students. But to go to another level in relationships—to become a multiplier—one must be intentional, strategic, and skilled. The greater the talent and resources a person possesses, the greater his potential to become a multiplier.

I am fortunate. I have a lot of multipliers in my life, highly gifted people who want to see me succeed, people such as Todd Duncan, Rick Goad, and Tom Mullins. Each of these men has a servant's heart. They are tops in their fields. They value partnership. They're always generating great ideas. And they're passionate about making a difference. They help me to sharpen my vision and maximize my strengths.

You probably have people like that in your life, people who live to help you succeed and have the skills to help you along the way. If you can think of people who have played the role of multiplier in your life, stop and take some time to call or write them and let them know what they've meant in your life.

4. Some People Divide Something in Life— We Avoid Them

R. G. LeTourneau, inventor of numerous kinds of heavy earthmoving equipment, says that his company used to make a scraper that was known as Model G. One day a customer asked a salesman what the *G* stood for. The salesman, like many people in his profession, was quick on his feet, and he replied, "The *G* stands for *gossip*, because like a talebearer, this machine moves a lot of dirt and moves it fast!"

Dividers are people who will really "take you to the basement," meaning they'll take you down as low as they can, as often as they can. They're like the company president who sent his personnel director a memo saying, "Search the organization for an alert, aggressive young man who could step into my shoes—and when you find him, fire him."

Dividers are so damaging because, unlike subtracters, their negative actions are usually intentional. They are hurtful people who make themselves look or feel better by trying to make someone else do worse than they do. As a result, they damage relationships and create havoc in people's lives.

TAKE OTHERS TO A HIGHER LEVEL

I believe that deep down everyone—even the most negative person—wants to be a lifter. We all want to be a positive influence in the lives of others. And we can be. If you want to lift people up and add value to their lives, keep the following in mind:

LIFTERS COMMIT THEMSELVES TO DAILY ENCOURAGEMENT

Roman philosopher Lucius Annaeus Seneca observed, "Wherever there is a human being, there is an opportunity for kindness." If you want to lift people up, take George Crane's advice. Encourage others, and do it daily.

LIFTERS KNOW THE LITTLE DIFFERENCE THAT SEPARATES HURTING AND HELPING

The little things you do every day have a greater impact on others than you might think. A smile, rather than a frown, can make someone's day. A kind word instead of criticism lifts an individual's spirits rather than dragging him down.

You hold the power to make another person's life better or worse by the things you do today. Those closest to you—your spouse, children, or parents—are most affected by what you say and do. Use that power wisely.

Lifters Initiate the Positive in a Negative Environment

It's one thing to be positive in a positive or neutral environment. It's another to be an instrument of change in a negative environment. Yet that's what lifters try to do. Sometimes that requires a kind word, other times it takes a servant's action, and occasionally it calls for creativity.

American revolutionary Ben Franklin told in his autobiography about asking a favor to create a positive connection in a negative environment. In 1736, Franklin was being considered for a position as clerk of the general assembly. Only one person stood in the way of his nomination, a powerful man who did not like Franklin.

Franklin wrote, "Having heard that he had in his library a certain very scarce book, I wrote a note to him, expressing my desire of perusing that book and requesting he would do me the favor of lending it to me." The man was flattered and delighted by the request. He loaned Franklin the book, and the two became lifelong friends.

LIFTERS UNDERSTAND LIFE IS NOT
A DRESS REHEARSAL

Here's a quote I've always loved: "I expect to pass through this world but once. Any good therefore that I can do, or any kindness that I can show to any fellow creature, let me do it now. Let me not defer or neglect it, for I shall not pass this way again."[2] People who lift others don't wait until tomorrow or some other "better" day to help people. They act now!

Everyone is capable of becoming a person who lifts up others. You don't have to be rich. You don't have to be a genius. You don't have to have it all together. You do have to care about people and initiate lifting activities. Don't let another day go by without lifting up the people in your life. Doing that will positively change the relationships you already have and open you up to many more.

6

Do Others
Find Me Trustworthy?

Trust is the foundation of all relationships.

I f you've traveled through smaller airports or have much experience flying in corporate aircraft, you've probably seen or flown in a Learjet. I've had the opportunity to fly in one a couple of times, and it's quite an experience. They're small—capable of carrying only five or six passengers—and very fast. It's like climbing into a narrow tube with jet engines strapped to it.

I have to admit, the whole experience of riding in a Learjet is pretty exhilarating. But by far the most amazing thing to me about it is the time it saves. I've traveled literally millions of miles on airlines, and I'm accustomed to long drives to airports, car rental returns, shuttles, terminal congestion, and seemingly endless delays. It can be a nightmare. Flying on a Learjet can easily cut travel time in half.

The father of this amazing airplane was a man named Bill Lear. An inventor, aviator, and business leader, Lear held more than 150 patents, including those of the automatic pilot, car radio, and eight-track tapes (you can't win them all). Lear was a pioneer in his thinking, and in the 1950s, he could see the potential for the manufacture of small corporate jets. It took him several years to make his dream a reality, but in 1963, the first Learjet made its maiden voyage, and in 1964 he delivered his first production jet to a client.

Lear's success was immediate, and he quickly sold many aircraft. But not long after he got his start, Lear learned that two aircraft he'd built had crashed under mysterious circumstances. He was devastated. At that time, fifty-five Learjets were privately owned, and Lear immediately sent word to all of the owners to ground their planes until he and his team could determine what had caused the crashes. The thought that more lives might be lost was far more important to him than any adverse publicity that action might generate in the media.

As he researched the ill-fated flights, Lear discovered a potential cause, but he couldn't verify the technical problem on the ground. There was only one sure way to find out whether he had diagnosed the problem correctly. He would have to try to re-create it personally—in the air.

It was a dangerous process, but that's what he did. As he flew the jet, he nearly lost control and almost met the same fate as the other two pilots. But he did manage to make it through the tests, and he was able to verify the defect. Lear developed a new part to correct the problem and fitted all fifty-five planes with it, eliminating the danger.

Grounding the planes cost Lear a lot of money. And it planted seeds of doubt in the minds of potential customers. As a result, he needed two years to rebuild the business. But Lear never regretted his decision. He was willing to risk his success, his fortune, and even his life to solve the mystery of those crashes—but not his integrity. And that takes character.

THE IMPORTANCE OF CHARACTER

How a person deals with the circumstances of life tells you many things about his character. Crisis doesn't necessarily make character, but it certainly does reveal it. Adversity is a crossroads that makes a person choose one of two paths:

character or compromise. Every time he chooses character, he becomes stronger, even if that choice brings negative consequences. As Nobel prize–winning author Alexander Solzhenitsyn noted, "The meaning of earthly existing lies, not as we have grown used to thinking, in prospering, but in the development of the soul." The development of character is at the heart of our development not just as leaders, but as human beings.

What must every person know about character?

1. Character Is More Than Talk

Anyone can *say* that he has integrity, but action is the real indicator of character. Your character determines who you are. Who you are determines what you see. What you see determines what you do. That's why you can never separate a person's character from his actions. If a person's actions and intentions are continually working against each other, then look to his character to find out why.

2. Talent Is a Gift, but Character Is a Choice

We have no control over a lot of things in life. We don't get to choose our parents. We don't select the location or circumstances of our birth and upbringing. We don't get to pick our talents or IQ. But we do choose our character. In fact, we create it every time we make choices—to cop out or dig out of a hard situation, to bend the truth or stand under the weight of it, to take the easy money or pay the price. As you live your life and make choices today, you are continuing to create your character.

3. Character Brings Lasting Success with People

True leadership always involves other people. (As the leadership proverb says, if you think you're leading and no one is following you, then you're only taking a walk.) Followers do not trust leaders whose character they know to be flawed, and they will not continue following them.

4. People Cannot Rise Above the Limitations of Their Character

Have you ever seen highly talented people suddenly fall apart when they achieved a certain level of success? The key to that phenomenon is character. Steven Berglas, a psychologist at Harvard Medical School and author of *The Success Syndrome,* says that people who achieve great heights but lack the bedrock character to sustain them through the stress are headed for disaster. He believes they are destined for one or more of the four As: *arrogance,* painful feelings of *aloneness,* destructive *adventure-seeking,* or *adultery.* Each is a terrible price to pay for weak character.

EXAMINE YOURSELF

If you've found yourself being sucked in by one of the four As that Berglas identifies, call a time-out. Do what you must to step away from some of the stress of your success, and seek professional help. Don't think that the valley you're in will pass with time, more money, or increased prestige. Unaddressed cracks in character only get deeper and more destructive with time.

If you're not struggling in any of these four areas, you should still examine the condition of your character. Ask yourself whether your words and actions match—all the time. When you say you'll finish an assignment, do you always follow through? If you tell your children that you'll make it to their recital or ball game, are you there for it? Can people trust your handshake as they would a legal contract?

As you lead others at home, at work, and in the community, recognize that your character is your most important asset. G. Alan Bernard, president of Mid Park, Inc., stated, "The respect that leadership must have requires that one's ethics be without question. A leader not only stays above the line between right and wrong, he stays well clear of the 'gray areas.'"

BUILDING CHARACTER

To improve your character, do the following:

SEARCH FOR THE CRACKS

Spend some time looking at the major areas of your life (work, marriage, family, service, etc.), and identify anywhere you might have cut corners, compromised, or let people down. Write down every instance you can recall from the past two months.

LOOK FOR PATTERNS

Examine the responses that you just wrote down. Is there a particular area where you have a weakness, or do you have a type of problem that keeps surfacing? Detectable patterns will help you diagnose character issues.

FACE THE MUSIC

The beginning of character repair comes when you face your flaws, apologize, and deal with the consequences of your actions. Create a list of people to whom you need to apologize for your actions; then follow through with sincere apologies.

REBUILD

It's one thing to face up to your past actions. It's another to build a new future. Now that you've identified any areas of weakness, create a plan that will prevent you from making the same mistakes again.

A man took his young daughter to a carnival, and she immediately ran over to a booth and asked for cotton candy. As the attendant handed her a huge ball of it, the father asked, "Sweetheart, are you sure you can eat all that?" "Don't worry, Dad," she answered, "I'm a lot bigger on the inside than on the outside."

That's what real character is—being bigger on the inside.

7

HOW SKILLED AM I
IN MY WORK?

To hit the mark, aim above it.

Benjamin Franklin always thought of himself as an ordinary citizen. One of seventeen children, Franklin was the son of a tradesman, a candlemaker, who was far from wealthy. He experienced a typical childhood. He attended school for only two years, and at age twelve, he was apprenticed to his brother in the printing trade.

Franklin worked hard and lived a simple life, governing his actions according to a set of thirteen virtues, upon which he graded himself daily. At age twenty he started his own printing business. Had Franklin been content to work at his trade, his name would be little more than a footnote in Philadelphia's history. Yet he lived an extraordinary life. He was one of the fathers of American independence and a great leader of the emerging nation. He coauthored the Declaration of Independence, and he later helped write the Treaty of Paris and the Constitution of the United States. (He was the only man who signed all three.) And he was selected to perform a difficult and dangerous secret diplomatic mission to Paris during the war to secure military and financial support for the Revolution.

What gave a Northern tradesman the opportunity to exert so much influence among the wealthy, predominately Southern landholders who headed the war for independence? I believe it was Franklin's incredible competence.

Benjamin Franklin excelled at everything he touched for seven decades. When he started his own printing business in 1726, people believed Philadelphia could not support a third printer, but Franklin quickly established a reputation as the most skilled and industrious printer in town. But the Philadelphia tradesman wasn't content with only that accomplishment.

Franklin's mind was curious, and he continually sought ways to improve himself and others. He expanded into publishing, his work including the noted *Poor Richard's Almanack*. He did extensive experiments with electricity and coined many of the terms still associated with its use. He invented numerous items such as the potbellied stove, the catheter, and bifocals. And when he traveled frequently across the Atlantic Ocean, he took it upon himself to chart the Gulf Stream. His attitude toward life could be seen in an aphorism he wrote for his almanac: "Hide not your talents. They for use were made. What's a sundial in the shade?"

The evidences of Franklin's talents were many. He helped establish Philadelphia's first library. He started the nation's first fire department. He developed the concept of daylight saving time. And he held many posts serving the government.

For the most part, Franklin was recognized for his ability. But sometimes he had to let his competence speak for itself. During a time when he was working on improvements in agriculture, he discovered that plaster made grains and grasses grow better, but he had a difficult time convincing his neighbors about the discovery. His solution? When spring arrived, he went to a field close to a path, dug out some letters into the dirt with his hands, put plaster into the ruts, and then sowed seed over the whole area. As people passed that way in following weeks, they could see green letters growing brighter than the rest of the field. They said simply, "This has been plastered." People got the message.

RAISE YOUR LEVEL
OF COMPETENCE

We all admire people who display high competence, whether they are precision craftsmen, world-class athletes, or successful business leaders. But the truth is that you don't have to be Fabergé, Michael Jordan, or Bill Gates to excel in the area of competence. If you want to cultivate that quality, here's what you need to do.

1. SHOW UP EVERY DAY

There's a saying, "All things come to him who waits." Unfortunately sometimes, it's just the leftovers from the people who got there first. Responsible people show up when they're expected. But highly competent people take it a step farther. They don't show up in body only. They come ready to play every day—no matter how they feel, what kind of circumstances they face, or how difficult they expect the game to be.

2. KEEP IMPROVING

Like Benjamin Franklin, all highly competent people continually search for ways to keep learning, growing, and improving. They do that by asking *why*. After all, the person who knows *how* will always have a job, but the person who knows *why* will always be the boss.

3. Follow Through with Excellence

I've never met a person I considered competent who didn't follow through. I bet it's the same for you. Willa A. Foster remarked, "Quality is never an accident; it is always the result of high intention, sincere effort, intelligent direction and skillful execution; it represents the wise choice of many alternatives." Performing at a high level of excellence is always a choice, an act of the will.

4. Accomplish More Than Expected

Highly competent people always go the extra mile. For them, good enough is never good enough. In *Men in Mid-Life Crisis*, Jim Conway writes that some people feel "a weakening of the need to be a great man and an increasing feeling of 'let's just get through this the best way we can.' Never mind hitting home runs. Let's just get through the ball game without getting beaned." Successful people cannot afford to have that kind of attitude. They need to do the job, and then some, day in and day out.

5. INSPIRE OTHERS

Highly competent people do more than perform at a high level. They inspire and motivate other people to do the same. While some rely on relational skills alone to survive, effective people combine these skills with high competence to take their organizations to new levels of excellence and influence.

HOW COMPETENT ARE YOU?

Where do you stand when it comes to getting the job done? Do you attack everything you do with fervor and perform at the highest level possible? Or is good enough sometimes good enough for you?

When you think about people who are competent, you're really considering only three types of people:

1. Those who can see what needs to happen.

2. Those who can make it happen.

3. Those who can make things happen when it really counts.

When it comes to your profession, where do you consistently perform? Are you a thinker, a doer, or a clutch player? The better you are, the greater potential for influence you will have with your people.

GETTING IN THE GAME

To improve your competence, do the following:

GET YOUR HEAD IN THE GAME

If you've been mentally or emotionally detached from your work, it's time to reengage. First, rededicate yourself to your job. Determine to give it an appropriate amount of your undivided attention. Second, figure out why you have been detached. Do you need new challenges? Are you in conflict with your boss or coworkers? Are you in a dead-end job? Identify the source of the problem, and create a plan to resolve it.

REDEFINE THE STANDARD

If you're not performing at a consistently high level, reexamine your standards. Are you shooting too low? Do you cut corners? If so, hit your mental reset button, and outline more demanding expectations for yourself.

FIND THREE WAYS TO IMPROVE

Nobody keeps improving without being intentional about it. Do a little research to find three things you can do to improve your professional skills. Then dedicate the time and money to follow through on them.

I read an editorial in *Texas Business* not long ago that said, "We are truly the lost generation, huffing and puffing down the fast track to nowhere, always looking to the dollar sign for direction. That's the only standard we recognize. We have no built-in beliefs, no ethical boundaries."

You're only as good as your private standards. When was the last time you gave a task your absolute best even though nobody but you would know about it?

8

Do I Keep Going
When Others Don't?

Quitters never win and winners never quit.

In the summer of 2001, my wife, Margaret, and I went to England for ten days with our friends Dan and Patti Reiland, Tim and Pam Elmore, and Andy Steimer. We've been close to the Reilands and Elmores about twenty years, and we've done a lot of traveling together, so we were really looking forward to the trip. And though we haven't known Andy nearly as long, he's become a good friend—and he's been to England so many times that he was acting almost like our unofficial tour guide.

As we prepared for the trip, several of us had specific interests and historic sites we wanted to include. For instance, I wanted to visit all the places related to John Wesley, the renowned evangelist of the eighteenth century. For more than thirty years, I've studied Wesley, read all his writings, and collected his books. So we went to Epworth, where he grew up, to Wesley's Chapel in London, and to many of the places where he preached. For Tim, we visited Cambridge and other sites related to apologist, professor, and author C. S. Lewis. Andy had only one must-see place on his list, since he had been to England so many times: Winston Churchill's war rooms.

Three of us wanted to walk in the places where our heroes had walked, to get a glimpse of history and maybe understand the sense of destiny one of these great leaders or thinkers must have experienced. Then there was Dan. Sure, Dan enjoyed sharing our interests. He loves the subject of leadership, he's read C. S. Lewis's works, and he is ordained as a Wesleyan pastor. And he had a great time visiting our preferred sites. But the one place he absolutely *had* to see was the crosswalk where the Beatles had been photographed for the *Abbey Road* album. Dan wanted us to get our picture taken walking across the street, just as John, Ringo, Paul, and George had.

Now, I like the Beatles, and I thought it might be fun to visit the site. But to Dan, it was more than a big deal. It was essential. If we didn't make it to Abbey Road, then his trip just wouldn't have been complete. Because of that, every day as we set out from our London hotel on our itinerary, Dan would press us intently: "Now, guys, we're going to make it to Abbey Road, right?"

On the last day, we were scheduled to finally make our Abbey Road trek. Everyone except Margaret got up at six o'clock and piled into two cabs to make the trip across town to the street outside the recording studio where the Beatles recorded their last album. Dan was so excited that I thought he was going to bounce off the walls of the cab.

When we got there, we couldn't believe it. The street was closed! Big construction trucks were everywhere, and orange cones filled the crosswalk. It looked as if we had made the trip for nothing. Because we would be leaving London later that afternoon, we wouldn't get another opportunity for the picture. Dan would have to go home empty handed.

We decided to get out of the cabs anyway, just to check out the situation. We figured there might be heavy construction occurring on the tiny street. However, we discovered that a huge crane, which was located about a half mile away, was scheduled to come down the street sometime in the afternoon, and that's why the road was closed. That gave me hope that we might succeed after all. None of us wanted

Dan to be disappointed, and I always love a challenge. So we went to work.

We struck up a conversation with the workmen who had closed the road. At first, they had no idea what we wanted. Then when they understood why we were there, they folded their arms, stood as solid as the Rock of Gibraltar, and told us it couldn't be done. It was their turf, it was their job, and they were not going to move. However, I did have to laugh when we talked to one worker who was about twenty-five years old. When we said that Dan wanted a photo like the one on the Beatles' album, and that the original had been taken on that very spot, the young man said, "Really? It was here?"

We talked to the guys some more. We joked. We offered to take them all out to lunch. And we told them how far we had come and how much the whole thing meant to Dan. "You can be Dan's heroes," I explained. After a while, I could see they were beginning to soften. Finally a big, burly guy with a thick accent said, "Oh, let's help the Yanks out. What could it hurt?"

The next thing we knew, it was like they were working for us. They began clearing cones and moving trucks. They even let Patti, Dan's wife, climb up onto one of the trucks to take the picture so that it would be from the same angle as the Beatles' original shot. Quickly we lined up: first Tim, then Andy, then me (with my shoes off like Paul McCartney), and finally Dan. It was a moment we won't soon forget, and the photo sits on my desk today to remind me of it.

WORKING WITH PERSISTENCE

On that summer day in London, did we succeed because of extraordinary talent? No. Was it because of our timing? Certainly not, since our timing got us into trouble in the first place. Was it power or sheer numbers? No, there were only six of us. We succeeded because we were tenacious. Our desire to get that picture was so strong that success for our little team was almost inevitable.

It's appropriate to finish the discussion of the essential qualities of a team player by talking about tenacity because tenacity is crucial to success. Even people who lack talent and fail to cultivate some of the other vital qualities of a team player have a chance to contribute to the team and help it succeed if they possess a tenacious spirit.

Being tenacious means . . .

1. GIVING ALL THAT YOU HAVE, NOT MORE THAN YOU HAVE

Some people who lack tenacity do so because they mistakenly believe that being tenacious demands from them more than they have to offer. As a result, they don't push themselves. However, being tenacious requires that you give 100 percent—not more, but certainly not less. If you give your all, you afford yourself every opportunity possible for success.

Look at the case of General George Washington. During the entire course of the Revolutionary War, he won only three battles. But he gave all he had, and when he did win, it counted. British general Cornwallis, who surrendered to Washington at Yorktown to end the war, said to the American commander, "Sir, I salute you not only as a great leader of men, but as an indomitable Christian gentleman who wouldn't give up."

2. WORKING WITH DETERMINATION, NOT WAITING ON DESTINY

Tenacious people don't rely on luck, fate, or destiny for their success. And when conditions become difficult, they keep working. They know that trying times are no time to quit trying. And that's what makes the difference. For the thousands of people who give up, there is always someone like Thomas Edison, who remarked, "I start where the last man left off."

3. QUITTING WHEN THE JOB IS DONE, NOT WHEN YOU'RE TIRED

Robert Strauss stated that "success is a little like wrestling a gorilla. You don't quit when you're tired—you quit when the gorilla is tired." If you want your team to succeed, you have to keep pushing beyond what you *think* you can do and find out what you're really capable of. It's not the first but the last step in the relay race, the last shot in the basketball game, the last yard with the football into the end zone that makes the difference, for that is where the game is won. Motivational author Napoleon Hill summed it up: "Every successful person finds that great success lies just beyond the point when they're convinced their idea is not going to work." Tenacity hangs on until the job is finished.

How tenacious are you? When others have given up, do you keep hanging on? If it's the bottom of the ninth inning and there are two outs, have you already lost the game mentally, or are you ready to rally the team to victory? If the team hasn't found a solution to a problem, are you willing to keep plugging away to the very end in order to succeed? If you sometimes give up before the rest of the team does, you may need a strong dose of tenacity.

How to Become More Tenacious

A. L. Williams says, "You beat 50 percent of the people in America by working hard. You beat another 40 percent by being a person of honesty and integrity and standing for something. The last 10 percent is a dogfight in the free enterprise system." To improve your tenacity . . .

Work harder and/or smarter

If you tend to be a clock-watcher who never works beyond quitting time no matter what, then you need to change your habits. Put in an additional sixty to ninety minutes of work every day by arriving at work thirty to forty-five minutes early and staying an equal amount of time after your normal hours. If you are someone who already puts in an inordinate number of hours, then spend more time planning to make your working hours more efficient.

STAND FOR SOMETHING

To succeed, you must act with absolute integrity. However, if you can add to that the power of purpose, you will possess an additional edge. Write on an index card how your day-to-day work relates to your overall purpose. Then review that card daily to keep your emotional fires burning.

MAKE YOUR WORK A GAME

Nothing feeds tenacity like our natural competitive nature. Try to harness that by making your work a game. Find others in your organization who have similar goals and create a friendly competition with them to motivate you and them.

ACCOMPLISHING THE IMPOSSIBLE

People said it couldn't be done—building a railroad from sea level on the coast of the Pacific Ocean into the Andes Mountains, the second-highest mountain range on earth after the Himalayans. Yet that is what Ernest Malinowski, a Polish-born engineer, wanted to do. In 1859, he proposed building a rail line from Callao on the coast of Peru into the country's interior—to an elevation of more than fifteen thousand feet. If he was successful, it would be the highest railway in the world.

The Andes are treacherous mountains. The altitude makes work difficult, but add to that frigid conditions, glaciers, and the potential for volcanic activity. And the mountains climb from sea level to tens of thousands of feet in a very short distance. Climbing to high altitude in the jagged mountains would require switchbacks, zigzags, and numerous bridges and tunnels.

But Malinowski and his work crews succeeded. Jans S. Plachta states, "There are approximately 100 tunnels and bridges, some of which are major engineering feats. It is difficult to visualize how this task could have been accomplished with relatively primitive construction equipment, high altitudes, and mountainous terrain as obstacles." The railroad still stands today as a testament to the tenacity of the men who built it. No matter what happened to them during the process, Malinowski and his team never, never, never quit.

9

AM I STRIVING
TO KEEP LEARNING?

*The day you stop growing is the beginning
of the end of your success.*

I f you see the image of a little man sporting a tiny moustache, carrying a cane, and wearing baggy pants, big, clumsy shoes, and a derby hat, you know immediately that it's Charlie Chaplin. Just about everyone recognizes him. In the 1910s and 1920s, he was *the* most famous and recognizable person on the planet. If we looked at today's celebrities, the only person even in the same category as Chaplin in popularity would be Michael Jordan. And to measure who is the bigger star, we would have to wait another seventy-five years to find out how well everyone remembers Michael.

When Chaplin was born, nobody would have predicted great fame for him. Born into poverty as the son of

English music hall performers, he found himself on the street as a small child when his mother was institutionalized. After years in workhouses and orphanages, he began working on the stage to support himself. By age seventeen, he was a veteran performer. In 1914, while just in his mid-twenties, he worked for Mack Sennett at Keystone Studios in Hollywood making $150 a week. During that first year in the movie business, he made thirty-five films working as an actor, writer, and director. Everyone recognized his talent immediately, and his popularity grew. A year later, he earned $1,250 a week. Then in 1918, he did something unheard-of. He signed the entertainment industry's first $1 million contract. He was rich; he was famous; and he was the most powerful filmmaker in the world—at the ripe old age of twenty-nine.

Chaplin was successful because he had great talent and incredible drive. But those traits were fueled by teachability. He continually strived to grow, learn, and perfect his craft. Even when he was the most popular and highest-paid performer *in the world*, he wasn't content with the status quo.

Chaplin explained his desire to improve to an interviewer:

When I am watching one of my pictures presented to an audience, I always pay close attention to what they don't laugh at. If, for example, several audiences do not laugh at a stunt I mean to be funny, I at once begin to tear that trick to pieces and try to discover what was wrong in the idea or in the execution of it. If I hear a slight ripple at something I had not expected to be funny, I ask myself why that particular thing got a laugh.

That desire to grow made him successful economically, and it brought a high level of excellence to everything he did. In those early days, Chaplin's work was hailed as marvelous entertainment. As time went by, he was recognized as a comic genius. Today many of his movies are considered masterpieces, and he is appreciated as one of the greatest filmmakers of all time. Screenwriter and film critic James Agee wrote, "The finest pantomime, the deepest emotion, the richest and most poignant poetry were in Chaplin's work."

If Chaplin had replaced his teachability with arrogant self-satisfaction when he became successful, his name would be right up there along with Ford Sterling or Ben Turpin, stars of silent films who are all but forgotten today. But Chaplin kept growing and learning as an actor, director, and eventually film executive. When he learned from experience that filmmakers were at the mercy of studios and distributors, he started his own organization, United Artists, along with Douglas Fairbanks, Mary Pickford, and D. W. Griffith. The film company is still in business today.

KEEP MOVING!

Successful people face the danger of contentment with the *status quo*. After all, if a successful person already possesses influence and has achieved a level of respect, why should he keep growing? The answer is simple:

Your growth determines who you are.
Who you are determines who you attract.
Who you attract determines the success of your
    organization.

If you want to grow your organization, *you* have to remain teachable.

Allow me to give you five guidelines to help you cultivate and maintain a teachable attitude:

1. CURE YOUR DESTINATION DISEASE

Ironically, lack of teachability is often rooted in achievement. Some people mistakenly believe that if they can accomplish a particular goal, they no longer have to grow. It can happen with almost anything: earning a degree, reaching a desired position, receiving a particular award, or achieving a financial goal.

But effective people cannot afford to think that way. The day they stop growing is the day they forfeit their potential—and the potential of the organization. Remember the words of Ray Kroc: "As long as you're green, you're growing. As soon as you're ripe, you start to rot."

2. OVERCOME YOUR SUCCESS

Another irony of teachability is that success often hinders it. Effective people know that what got them there doesn't keep them there. If you have been successful in the past, beware. And consider this: if what you did yesterday still looks big to you, you haven't done much today.

3. SWEAR OFF SHORTCUTS

My friend Nancy Dornan says, "The longest distance between two points is a shortcut." That's really true. For everything of value in life, you pay a price. As you desire to grow in a particular area, figure out what it will really take, including the price, and then determine to pay it.

4. TRADE IN YOUR PRIDE

Teachability requires us to admit we don't know everything, and that can make us look bad. In addition, if we keep learning, we must also keep making mistakes. But as writer and expert craftsman Elbert Hubbard said, "The greatest mistake one can make in life is to be continually fearing you will make one." You cannot be prideful and teachable at the same time. Emerson wrote, "For everything you gain, you lose something." To gain growth, give up your pride.

5. NEVER PAY TWICE FOR THE SAME MISTAKE

Teddy Roosevelt asserted, "He who makes no mistakes, makes no progress." That's true. But the person who keeps making *the same* mistakes also makes no progress. As a teachable person, you will make mistakes. Forget them, but always remember what they taught you. If you don't, you will pay for them more than once.

When I was a kid growing up in rural Ohio, I saw this

sign in a feed store: "If you don't like the crop you are reaping, check the seed you are sowing." Though the sign was an ad for seeds, it contained a wonderful principle.

What kind of crop are you reaping? Do your life and leadership seem to be getting better day after day, month after month, year after year? Or are you constantly fighting just to hold your ground? If you're not where you hoped you would be by this time in your life, your problem may be lack of teachability. When was the last time you did something for the first time? When was the last time you made yourself vulnerable by diving into something for which you weren't the expert? Observe your attitude toward growing and learning during the next several days or weeks to see where you stand.

NEVER STOP GROWING

To improve your teachability, do the following:

OBSERVE HOW YOU REACT TO MISTAKES

Do you admit your mistakes? Do you apologize when appropriate? Or are you defensive? Observe yourself. And ask a trusted friend's opinion. If you react badly—or you make no mistakes at all—you need to work on your teachability.

TRY SOMETHING NEW

Go out of your way today to do something different that will stretch you mentally, emotionally, or physically. Challenges change us for the better. If you really want to start growing, make new challenges part of your daily activities.

LEARN IN YOUR AREA OF STRENGTH

Read six to twelve books a year on leadership or your field of specialization. Continuing to learn in an area where you are already an expert prevents you from becoming jaded and unteachable.

After winning his third world championship, bull rider Tuff Hedeman didn't have a big celebration. He moved on to Denver to start the new season—and the whole process over again. His comment: "The bull won't care what I did last week." Whether you're an untested rookie or a successful veteran, if you want to be a champion tomorrow, be teachable today.

PART III

SUCCESS AT THE NEXT LEVEL

10

Am I Willing to Do the Tough Jobs?

Successful people do the things that unsuccessful people are unwilling to do.

It's said that an aid group in South Africa once wrote to missionary and explorer David Livingstone, asking, "Have you found a good road to where you are? If so, we want to know how to send other men to join you."

Livingstone replied, "If you have men who will come only if they know there is a good road, I don't want them. I want men who will come even if there is no road at all." That's what top leaders want from the people working for them: they want individuals who are willing to do what others won't.

Few things gain the appreciation of a top leader more quickly than an employee with a whatever-it-takes attitude. That is what successful people must have. They must be willing and able to think outside of their job description, to be willing to tackle the kinds of jobs that others are too proud or too frightened to take on. These things are what often elevate successful people above their peers.

What It Means to Do What Others Won't

Perhaps you already possess a whatever-it-takes mind-set, and if a task is honest, ethical, and beneficial, you're willing to take it on. If so, good for you! Now all you need is to know how to direct that attitude into action so that you're doing the things that will make the greatest impact and create influence with others. Here are the top ten things I recommend you do to become a successful person and a good leader:

1. Successful People Take the Tough Jobs

The ability to accomplish difficult tasks earns others' respect very quickly. In *Developing the Leader Within You,* I point out that one of the quickest ways to gain leadership is problem solving.

Problems continually occur at work, at home, and in life in general. My observation is that people don't like problems, weary of them quickly, and will do almost anything to get away from them. This climate makes others place the reins of leadership into your hands—if you are willing and able to either tackle their problems or train them to solve them. Your problem-solving skills will always be needed because people always have problems.[1]

Not only does taking on tough jobs earn you respect, but it also helps you become a better leader. You learn resiliency and tenacity during tough assignments, not easy ones. When tough choices have to be made and results are difficult to achieve, leaders are forged.

2. SUCCESSFUL PEOPLE PAY THEIR DUES

Former U.S. senator Sam Nunn said, "You have to pay the price. You will find that everything in life exacts a price, and you will have to decide whether the price is worth the prize." To become a successful person, you will have to pay a price. You will have to give up other opportunities in order to lead. You will have to sacrifice some personal goals for the sake of others. You will have to get out of your comfort zone and do things you've never done before. You will have to keep learning and growing when you don't feel like it. You will have to repeatedly put others ahead of yourself. And if you desire to be a really good leader, you will have to do these things without fanfare or complaint. But remember, as NFL legend George Halas said, "Nobody who ever gave their best ever regretted it."

3. Successful People Work in Obscurity

I think very highly of the importance of leadership. I guess that's obvious for a guy whose motto is "Everything rises and falls on leadership." Occasionally someone will ask me about how ego fits into the leadership equation. They'll want to know what keeps a leader from having a huge ego. I think the answer lies in each leader's pathway to leadership. If people paid their dues and gave their best in obscurity, ego is usually not a problem.

One of my favorite examples of this occurred in the life of Moses in the Old Testament. Though born a Hebrew, he lived a life of privilege in the palace of Egypt until he was forty years old. But after killing an Egyptian, he was exiled to the desert for forty years. There God used him as a shepherd and father, and after four decades of faithful service in obscurity, Moses was called to leadership. Scripture says by that time he was the most humble man in the world. Bill Purvis, the senior pastor of a large church in Columbus, Georgia, said, "If you do what you can, with what you have, where you are, then God won't leave you where you are, and He will increase what you have."

English novelist and poet Emily Bronte said, "If I could I would always work in silence and obscurity, and let my efforts be known by their results." Not everyone wants to be out of the spotlight as she did. But it's important for a leader to learn to work in obscurity because it is a test of personal integrity. The key is being willing to do something because it matters, not because it will get you noticed.

4. Successful People Succeed with Difficult People

People working at the bottom of an organization usually have no choice concerning whom they work with. As a result, they often have to work with difficult people. In contrast, people at the top almost never have to work with difficult people because they get to choose who they work with. If someone they work with becomes difficult, they often let that person go or move him or her out.

For leaders in the middle, the road is different. They have some choice in the matter, but not complete control. They may not be able to get rid of difficult people, but they can often avoid working with them. But good leaders— ones who learn to lead up, across, and down—find a way to succeed with people who are hard to work with. Why do they do it? Because it benefits the organization. How do they do it? They work at finding common ground and connect with them. And instead of putting these difficult people in their place, they try to put themselves in their place.

5. SUCCESSFUL PEOPLE PUT THEMSELVES ON THE LINE

If you want to be successful, you must distinguish yourself from your colleagues. How do you do that, especially while paying your dues or working in obscurity? One way is to take a risk. You cannot play it safe and stand out at the same time.

Here's the tricky thing about taking risks when you work in organization. You should never be casual about risking what's not yours. I call that "betting with other people's money." You don't have the right to put the organization on the line. Nor would it be right for you to create high risk for others in the organization. If you are going to take a risk, you need to put *yourself* on the line. Play it smart, but don't play it safe.

6. SUCCESSFUL PEOPLE ADMIT FAULTS BUT NEVER MAKE EXCUSES

It's easier to move from failure to success than from excuses to success. And you will have greater credibility with your leader if you admit your shortcomings and refrain from making excuses. I guarantee that. Of course, that doesn't mean you don't need to produce results. Baseball coach and tutor McDonald Valentine said, "The higher the level you play, the less they accept excuses."

A good time to make mistakes and learn is before you are recognized by others as successful. That's when you want to discover your identity and work things out. You can discover your leadership strengths before you have a leadership position. If you fall short in an area, you can work to overcome your mistakes. If you keep falling short in the same way, you may learn how to overcome an obstacle, or you may discover an area of weakness where you will need to collaborate with others. But no matter what, don't make excuses. Steven Brown, president of the Fortune Group, summed up this issue: "Essentially there are two actions in life: performance and excuses. Make a decision as to which you will accept from yourself."

7. SUCCESSFUL PEOPLE DO MORE THAN EXPECTED

Expectations are high for people at the top. And, unfortunately, in many organizations the expectations for people at the bottom are low. But expectations are mixed in the middle of an organization. So if you work in an organization and you do more than is expected of you, you stand out, and often there can be wonderful, serendipitous results.

When Chris Hodges, a senior pastor who is a donor and volunteer trainer with EQUIP, was working as a staff member at a large church in Baton Rouge, his boss, Larry Stockstill, had the opportunity to become the host of a live television show. Chris had no responsibilities related to the show, and was, in fact, rather low in the organization's hierarchy. But he knew that the show was important to Larry, so Chris took it upon himself to go down to the studio to see the first taping. As it turned out, he was the only staff member to do so.

There was great excitement in the studio as the hour of the first broadcast approached. That excitement quickly turned to panic when the guest who was scheduled to appear on the show called in to say he was having a problem getting there. The guest wasn't worried, because he thought they could just start the taping later. What he didn't realize was that the show was scheduled to go on the air live!

In that moment, Larry looked around, saw Chris, and said, "You're going to be my guest today." The crew scrambled, put a microphone on Chris, slapped some makeup on his face, and sat him down in the chair next to Larry. Then to Chris's great shock, when the lights turned on and the cameras started rolling, Larry introduced Chris as his cohost.

Chris ended up being on that show with Larry every week for two and a half years. The experience changed him forever. Not only did it build his relationship with his leader, but it also made him well-known in the community. More importantly, he learned to think on his feet and become a better communicator, skills that serve him well every day of his life. And it all happened because he decided to do more than was expected of him.

8. Successful People Are the First to Step Up and Help

In *25 Ways to Win with People,* I point out that being the first to help others is a great way to make them feel like a million bucks. It lets them know you care. The kind of influence you gain from helping a peer is also gained with your leader when you step up and help others. Haven't you found the following to be true?

- The first person to volunteer is a hero and is given the "10" treatment.
- The second person is considered a helper and viewed as only slightly above average.
- The third person, along with everyone after, is seen as a follower and is ignored.

It doesn't matter whom you're helping, whether it's your boss, a peer, or someone working for you. When you help someone on the team, you help the whole team. And when you help the team, you're helping your leaders. And that gives them reasons to notice and appreciate you.

9. SUCCESSFUL PEOPLE PERFORM TASKS THAT ARE "NOT THEIR JOB"

Few things are more frustrating for a leader than having someone refuse to do a task because it is "not his job." (In moments like those, most of the top leaders I know are tempted to invite such people to be without a job altogether!) Successful people don't think in those terms. They understand the Law of the Big Picture from *The 21 Irrefutable Laws of Leadership*: "The goal is more important than the role."

A successful person's goal is to get the job done, to fulfill the vision of the organization and its leader. That often means doing whatever it takes. As a leader "moves up," that more often takes the form of hiring someone to get it done, but leaders in the middle often don't have that option. So instead, they jump in and get it done themselves.

10. Successful People Take Responsibility for Their Responsibilities

I recently saw a cartoon where a dad is reading a book to his little boy at bedtime. The title on the cover of the book says, *The Story of Job*, and the boy has only one question for his father: "Why didn't he sue someone?"

Isn't that the way a lot of people think these days? Their knee-jerk reaction to adversity is to blame someone else. That's not the case with successful people. They take hold of their responsibilities and follow through with them 100 percent.

Lack of responsibility can be a deal breaker when it comes to the people who work for me. When my employees don't get the job done, certainly I become disappointed. But I'm willing to work with them to help them improve—if they are taking responsibility for themselves. I know they will work at getting better if they take ownership and have teachable spirits. We have no starting point for improvement, however, if they don't get the job done and they fail to take responsibility. In such cases, it's time to move on and find someone else to take their place.

WHAT ARE YOU WILLING TO DO?

J. C. Penney said, "Unless you are willing to drench yourself in your work beyond the capacity of the average man, you are just not cut out for positions at the top." I'd say that you're not cut out for leadership in the middle either! People who want to be effective are willing to do what others won't. And because of that, their leaders are willing to resource them, promote them, and be influenced by them.

11

Am I Ready to
Step Up My Game?

Successful people become go-to players.

The Law of the Catalyst in *The 17 Indisputable Laws of Teamwork* states that winning teams have players who make things happen. That's always true—whether in sports, business, government, or some other arena. Those team members who can make things happen are their go-to players. They demonstrate consistent competence, responsibility, and dependability.

Successful Teams Have
Go-To Players

Everyone admires go-to players and looks to them when the heat is on—not only their leaders, but also their followers and peers. When I think of go-to players, I mean people who always produce.

1. GO-TO PLAYERS PRODUCE WHEN THE PRESSURE'S ON

There are many different kinds of people in the workplace, and you can measure them according to what they do for the organization:

WHAT THEY DO	KIND OF PLAYER
Never deliver	Detrimental
Sometimes deliver	Average
Always deliver when in their comfort zone	Valuable
Always deliver regardless of the situation	Invaluable

Go-to players are the people who find a way to make things happen no matter what. They don't have to be in familiar surroundings. They don't have to be in their comfort zones. The circumstances don't have to be fair or favorable. The pressure doesn't hinder them either. In fact, if anything, the more pressure there is, the better they like it. They always produce when the heat is on.

2. GO TO PLAYERS PRODUCE WHEN THE RESOURCES ARE FEW

In 2004 when *Today Matters* came out and I was frequently being asked to speak on the subject, I was once booked to do back-to-back sessions in Little Rock, Arkansas. After the first session, the site ran out of books. When the leader of the organization I was speaking for found out, he mobilized some of his people and sent them out to all the bookstores in town to buy more copies of the book so that his people could have access to them right after my second speaking session. I think he ended up buying every copy in town.

The thing I loved about it was that he wanted his people to benefit from the book, and he knew that if he didn't have it there after I spoke, they probably wouldn't get a copy. So he made it happen—even though he had to buy the books at full retail and resell them for that same amount. It took a lot of effort and provided no financial return. What a leader!

3. GO-TO PLAYERS PRODUCE WHEN THE MOMENTUM IS LOW

Organizations have only three kinds of people when it comes to momentum. There are momentum breakers—people who sabotage the leader or organization and actually sap momentum as a result. These people have terrible attitudes and represent the bottom 10 percent of the organization. (At General Electric, Jack Welch made it his goal every year to identify and fire these people.) The second group is comprised of the momentum takers—people who merely take things as they come. They neither create nor diminish momentum; they simply flow with it. These people represent the middle 80 percent.

The final group is the momentum makers—the people who move things forward and create momentum. These are the leaders in the organization and comprise the top 10 percent. These momentum makers make progress. They overcome obstacles. They help move others along. They actually create energy in the organization when the rest of the team is feeling tired or discouraged.

4. GO-TO PLAYERS PRODUCE WHEN THE LOAD IS HEAVY

Good employees always have the desire to be helpful to their leaders. I've worked with many of them over the years.

I always appreciate it when someone who works with me says, "I've finished my work. Can I do something for you?" But there is another level of play that some go-to players reach, and you can see it in their ability to carry a heavy load anytime their leader needs it. They don't help the leader with a heavy load only when theirs is light. They do it anytime their leader's load is heavy.

Linda Eggers, Tim Elmore, and Dan Reiland are examples of heavy load lifters for me. For years, when I've been pressed, they've taken tasks from me and completed them with excellence. Dan Reiland is so incredible at this that he continues to do it even now—and he doesn't even work for me anymore. He does it as a friend.

The keys to becoming this kind of player are availability and responsibility. Being a heavy load lifter is really an attitude issue, not a position issue. If you have the willingness and capacity to lift the load of your leaders when they need it, you will have influence with them.

5. Go-To Players Produce When the Leader Is Absent

The greatest opportunity for a leader in the middle of an organization to distinguish himself is when the leader is absent. It is at those times that a leadership vacuum exists, and leaders can rise up to fill it. True, when leaders know they will be absent, they usually designate a leader to stand in for them. But even then, there are still opportunities for people to step up, take responsibility, and shine.

If you step forward to lead when there is a leadership vacuum, you may have a very good chance of distinguishing yourself. You should also know, however, that when people step up to fill that vacuum, it almost always exposes their true colors. If their motives are good, and they desire to lead for the good of the organization, it will show through. If they are attempting a power grab for personal gain and their own advancement, that will show through too.

6. GO-TO PLAYERS PRODUCE WHEN THE TIME IS LIMITED

I love a sign I saw at a small business called "The 57 Rules to Deliver the Goods." Beneath the title it read:

Rule 1: Deliver the Goods
Rule 2: The Other 56 Don't Matter

That's the philosophy of go-to players. They deliver no matter how tough the situation is.

Look for Your Opportunity
to Step Up

As I was working on this chapter, Rod Loy told me a story about when he was a leader in the middle of an organization. At a large meeting, his leader announced a new program that he said was in place. Rod listened with interest, because he had not been aware of it. It sounded great, but then his leader announced that Rod would be leading the program, and anyone who was interested in it could talk to him about it after the meeting.

Rod had not been informed of his role in this program, but that didn't matter. During the rest of the meeting while his leader spoke, Rod quickly sketched out the design and action plan for the program. When the meeting was over and people approached him, he communicated his plan and launched it. Rod said it may not have been his best work, but it was good work under the circumstances. It created a win for the organization, preserved his leader's credibility, and served the people well.

You may never find yourself in the kind of situation Rod did. But if you adopt the positive attitude and tenacity of a go-to player, and take every opportunity to make things happen, you will probably perform as he did under similar circumstances. If you do, your leader will come to rely on you, and the people we rely on increase their influence and credibility every day we work with them.

12

Am I Ready to Lead
at the Next Level?

To reach the next level, lead others to success.

Growing organizations are always looking for good people to step up to the next level and lead. How do they find out if a person is qualified to make that jump? By looking at that person's track record in his or her current position. The key to moving up as an emerging leader is to focus on being successful where you are and leading well on that level, not on moving up the ladder. If you are successful where you are, I believe you will be given an opportunity to succeed at a higher level.

To Move Up, Learn to Lead

As you strive to become the most successful person you can be, keep the following things in mind:

1. Leadership Is a Journey That Starts Where You Are, Not Where You Want to Be

Recently, while I was driving in my car, a vehicle to the left of me attempted to turn right from the middle lane and caused an accident. Fortunately, I was able to slow down quickly and lessen the impact; but still, my air bags deployed, and both cars were greatly damaged.

The first thing I noticed after I stopped and took stock of the situation was that the little computer screen in my car was showing my exact location according to the GPS system. I stared at it a moment, wondering why the car was telling me my exact latitude and longitude. And then I thought, *Of course!* If you're in real trouble and you call for help, the first thing emergency workers will want to know is your location. You can't get anywhere until you first know where you are.

Leadership is similar. To know how to get where you want to go, you need to know where you are. To get where you want to go, you need to focus on what you're doing now. Award-winning sportswriter Ken Rosenthals said, "Each time you decide to grow again, you realize you are starting at the bottom of another ladder." You need to have your eyes fixed on your current responsibilities, not the ones you wish to have someday. I've never known a person focused on yesterday to have a better tomorrow.

2. LEADERSHIP SKILLS ARE THE SAME, BUT THE "LEAGUE OF PLAY" CHANGES

If you get promoted, don't think that because your new office is just a few feet down the hall from your old place that the difference is just a few steps. When you get "called up" to another level of leadership, the quality of your game must rise quickly.

No matter what level you're working on, leadership skills are needed at that level. Each new level requires a higher degree of skill. The easiest place to see this is in sports. Some players can make the jump from recreational league to high school. Fewer can make it from high school to college. And only a handful can make it to the professional level.

Your best chance of making it into the next "league of play" is to grow on the current level so that you will be able to go to the next level.

3. GREAT RESPONSIBILITIES COME ONLY AFTER HANDLING SMALL ONES WELL

When I teach at a conference or go to a book signing, people sometimes confide in me that they desire to write books too. "How do I get started?" they ask.

"How much writing do you do now?" I ask in return.

Some tell me about articles and other pieces they are

writing, and I simply encourage them; but most of the time they sheepishly respond, "Well, I haven't really written anything yet."

"Then you need to start writing," I explain. "You've got to start small and work up to it."

Leadership is the same. You've got to start small and work up to it. A person who has never led before needs to try to influence one other person. Someone who has some influence should try to build a team. Just start with what's necessary.

St. Francis of Assisi said, "Start doing what is necessary; then do what is possible; and suddenly you are doing the impossible." All good leadership begins where you are. It was Napoleon who said, "The only conquests which are permanent and leave no regrets are our conquests over ourselves." The small responsibilities you have before you now comprise the first great leadership conquest you must make. Don't try to conquer the world until you've taken care of things in your own backyard.

4. LEADING AT YOUR CURRENT LEVEL CREATES YOUR RÉSUMÉ FOR GOING TO THE NEXT LEVEL

When you go to see a doctor for the first time, you are usually asked a lot of questions about your family history. In fact, there are usually more questions about that than there are about your lifestyle. Why? Because family history, more than anything else, seems to be what determines your health.

When it comes to leadership success, history is also similarly disproportionate. Your track record where you work now is what leaders will look at when trying to decide if you can do a job. I know that when I interview someone for a job, I put 90 percent of the emphasis on the track record.

If you want to get the chance to lead on another level, then your best chance for success is to lead well where you are now. Every day that you lead and succeed, you are building a résumé for your next job.

5. WHEN YOU CAN LEAD VOLUNTEERS WELL, YOU CAN LEAD ALMOST ANYONE

At a recent President's Day conference where we were discussing leadership development, a CEO asked me, "How can I pick the best leader out of a small group of leaders? What do I look for?"

There are many things that indicate someone has leadership potential—the ability to make things happen, strong people skills, vision, desire, problem-solving skills, self-discipline, a strong work ethic. But there is one really great test of leadership that is almost foolproof, and that is what I suggested: "Ask them to lead a volunteer group."

If you want to test your own leadership, then try leading volunteers. Why is that so difficult? Because with volunteers, you have no leverage. It takes every bit of leadership skill you have to get people who don't have to do anything to do what you ask. If you're not challenging enough, they lose interest. If you push too hard, they drop out. If your people skills are weak, they won't spend any time with you. If you cannot communicate the vision, they won't know where to go or why.

If you lead others and your organization has any kind of community service focus, encourage the people on your team to volunteer. Then watch to see how they do. If they thrive in that environment, then you know that they possess many of the qualifications to go to another level in your organization.

LIVING ON THE NEXT LEVEL

Donald McGannon, former CEO of Westinghouse Broadcasting Corporation, stated, "Leadership is action, not position." Taking action—and helping others to do the same in a coordinated effort—is the essence of leadership. Do those things where you are, and you won't remain long there.

NOTES

Chapter 3

1. Robert M. McMath and Thom Forbes, *What Were They Thinking?* (New York: Random House, 1998).

2. Patricia Sellers, "Now Bounce Back!" *Fortune* (May 1, 1995), 50–51.

Chapter 4

1. Tommy Franks and Malcolm McConnell, *American Soldier* (New York: Regan Books, 2004), 99.

2. Jim Collins, *Good to Great* (New York: Harper Business, 2001), 139.

Chapter 5

1. Ella Wheeler Wilcox, "Which Are You?" *Custer, and Other Poems* (Chicago: W. B. Conkey Company, 1896), 134.

2. Anonymous.

Chapter 10

1. John C. Maxwell, *Developing the Leader Within You* (Nashville: Thomas Nelson, 1993), 75–76.

About the Author

John C. Maxwell is an internationally recognized leadership expert, speaker, and author who has sold over 16 million books. His organizations have trained more than 2 million leaders worldwide. Dr. Maxwell is the founder of EQUIP and INJOY Stewardship Services. Every year he speaks to Fortune 500 companies, international government leaders, and audiences as diverse as the United States Military Academy at West Point, the National Football League, and ambassadors at the United Nations. A *New York Times*, *Wall Street Journal*, and *Business Week* best-selling author, Maxwell was named the World's Top Leadership Guru by Leadershipgurus.net. He was also one of only 25 authors and artists named to Amazon.com's 10th Anniversary Hall of Fame. Three of his books, *The 21 Irrefutable Laws of Leadership*, *Developing the Leader Within You*, and *The 21 Indispensable Qualities of a Leader* have each sold over a million copies.

BOOKS BY DR. JOHN C. MAXWELL
CAN TEACH YOU HOW TO BE A REAL SUCCESS

RELATIONSHIPS

Encouragement Changes Everything
25 Ways to Win With People
Winning With People
Relationships 101
The Treasure of a Friend
The Power of Partnership in the Church
Becoming a Person of Influence
Be A People Person
The Power of Influence
Ethics 101

ATTITUDE

Success 101
The Difference Maker
The Journey From Success to Significance
Attitude 101
Failing Forward
Your Bridge to a Better Future
Living at the Next Level
The Winning Attitude
Be All You Can Be
The Power of Thinking Big
Think on These Things
The Power of Attitude
Thinking for a Change

EQUIPPING

The Choice Is Yours
Mentoring 101
Talent is Never Enough
Equipping 101
Developing the Leaders Around You
The 17 Essential Qualities of a Team Player
Success One Day at a Time
The 17 Indisputable Laws of Teamwork
Your Road Map for Success
Today Matters
Partners in Prayer

LEADERSHIP

Leadership Promises For Your Work Week
Leadership Gold
Go for Gold
*The 21 Most Powerful Minutes
in a Leader's Day*

Revised & Updated 10th Anniversary
Edition of *The 21 Irrefutable
Laws of Leadership*

The 360 Degree Leader
Leadership Promises for Every Day
Leadership 101
The Right to Lead
The 21 Indispensable Qualities of a Leader
Developing the Leader Within You
The Power of Leadership